Irresistible Ice Pops

Sunil Vijayakar

Irresistible
Ice Pops

Sunil Vijayakar

First published in 2012

LOVE FOOD is an imprint of Parragon Books Ltd

Parragon
Queen Street House
4 Queen Street
Bath BA1 1HE, UK

www.parragon.com

ISBN: 978-1-4454-7776-3

Printed in China

Created and produced by Pene Parker and Becca Spry
Author and home economist: Sunil Vijayakar
Photographer: Karen Thomas

Notes for the Reader

This book uses standard kitchen measuring spoons and cups. All spoon and cup measurements are level
unless otherwise indicated. Unless otherwise stated, milk is assumed to be whole, eggs are large and individual
fruits are medium.

The times given are only an approximate guide. Preparation times differ according to the techniques used by different
people and the cooking times may also vary from those given. Optional ingredients, variations, or serving suggestions
have not been included in the calculations.

Recipes using raw or very lightly cooked eggs should be avoided by infants, the elderly, pregnant women, and people
with weakened immune systems. Pregnant and breast-feeding women are advised to avoid eating peanuts and peanut
products. People with nut allergies should be aware that some of the prepared ingredients used in the recipes in this
book may contain nuts. Always check the packaging before use.

Contents

Making Your Own Ice Pops

It all started in San Francisco in 1905, when an 11-year-old boy, Frank Epperson, accidentally left a mixture of sweetened club soda in a cup, with a stirring stick, out on his porch. It was a freezing night and Frank awoke the next morning to discover a frozen "ice pop."

The rest is history, and now ice pops come in all shapes, flavors, colors, and sizes. The simplest ones are fruit juice-based, and the more elaborate ones have many layers of flavor and color.

You and your children can make wonderful ice pops with different flavors, textures, and shapes with the minimum of equipment. It's a great way to get kids involved in cooking and excited about creating their own flavors.

Sugar Syrup

You can make ice pops from almost any fruit or flavoring, but there are some things you should consider when it comes to freezing them. The secret to making most ice pops soft and smooth is the inclusion of a sugar syrup. This lowers the freezing point of a liquid and acts as a lubricant between the ice crystals. Dissolving or mixing it into the base ingredients will allow for the flavors to be distributed evenly and create a smooth and delicious treat. Here is the recipe for sugar syrup, which is easy to make.

Makes: 1 cup
Prep: 5 minutes
Cook: 9–12 minutes
Cool: 1 hour

* ½ cup superfine sugar
* 1 cup water

1. Put the sugar and water in a small saucepan. Cook over a low heat, stirring, for 6–8 minutes, or until all the sugar has dissolved.

2. Increase the heat to high until the mixture comes to a boil, then reduce the heat to medium and simmer for 3–4 minutes.

3. Remove from the heat, cover, and let stand until completely cooled.

4. Store the cooled syrup in a sealed container in the refrigerator for up to a week.

Equipment

Ice pops are so easy to make that you will require little in the way of equipment. Apart from ice pop molds and sticks, the most important thing you'll need is a blender, which you can use to puree fruit mixtures for the recipes. If you want pureed fruit to have a silky smooth consistency, you will also need a metal strainer to scrape the mixture through before discarding the seeds. And, of course, you need a freezer!

Ice Pop Molds

You can get an amazing variety of ice pop molds online, in supermarkets, and in good kitchen stores. They come in various shapes and sizes. However, you don't have to buy special molds; instead, be creative and use other freezable containers, such as metal molds, ramekins (individual ceramic dishes), mini tart pans, small paper cups, recycled yogurt containers, or any short or narrow plastic glass. Remember that the top of a mold should be wider than, or the same diameter as, the rest of it, so the ice pops can be unmolded easily.

Ice Pop Sticks

Most store-bought ice pop molds come with a built-in ice pop stick. You can also buy wooden ice pop sticks from craft stores or on-line. Buy them in bulk, because they will be less expensive and are great to have on hand for spontaneous ice pop making. If you don't have ice pop sticks, you can try other items, such as long cinnamon sticks or lemongrass stalks for an unusual twist.

Techniques and Tips

Inserting Ice Pop Sticks

If you are using store-bought molds with their own plastic sticks, follow the manufacturer's directions for inserting the sticks. If your molds don't come with sticks, use wooden ones. You will need a way to hold the sticks in place while your ice pop freezes. The easiest and most effective way is to cover the filled molds with aluminum foil and make a small slit with a sharp knife in the center. Insert the stick and it will be secure until your ice pop is frozen. If the ice pop mixture is very liquid, you might have to freeze the mixture for about an hour, or until it is slushy, before you insert the stick, then continue to freeze until solid.

Filling Ice Pop Molds

During freezing, the ingredients will expand, so be careful when filling the molds to leave at least a ¼–½-inch space at the top. Also keep in mind that some liquids, such as sodas and other carbonated beverages, have a high air content and will expand more than denser mixtures, such as pureed fruit, yogurt, and cream.

Alcohol in Ice Pops

Because alcohol freezes at a much lower temperature than water, don't use too much of it in your ice pop mixture or it will not freeze well. Pops containing alcohol are highlighted with this symbol and should be eaten only by adults.

Unmolding Ice Pops

There are two ways to unmold an ice pop: you can dip the frozen molds into warm water for a few seconds and gently release the pops while holding onto the sticks; alternatively, you can wrap the mold in a hot water-soaked dish towel until the pop can be unmolded.

"Do not restrict yourself to the recipes in this book… adapt them to suit your tastes and freeze up some fun in the kitchen!"

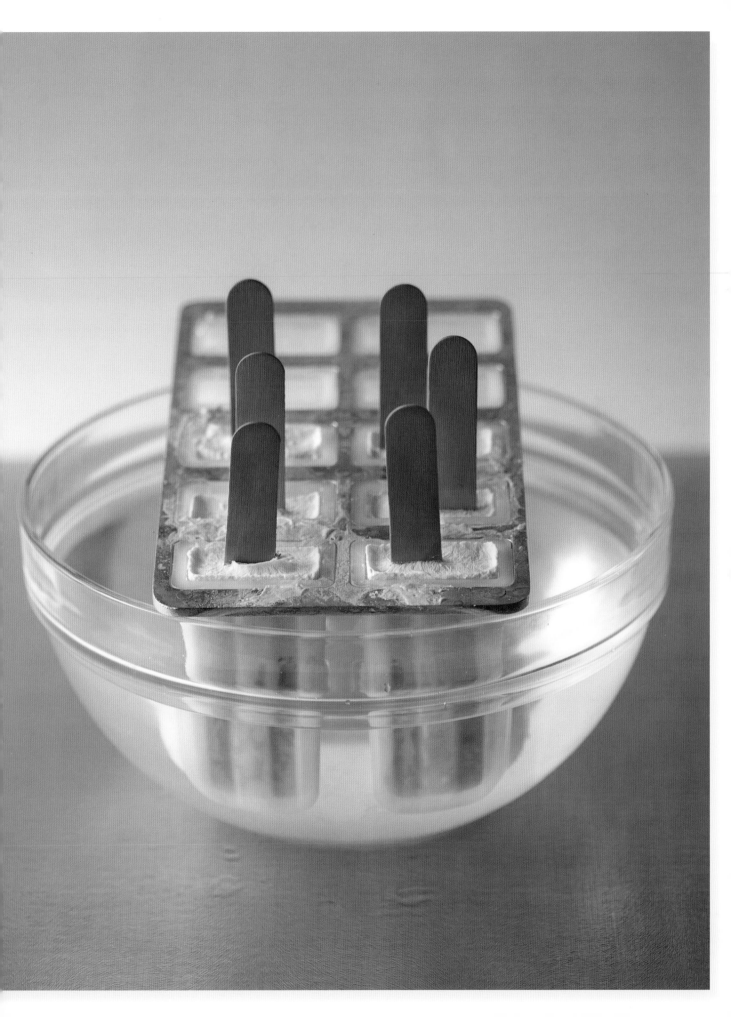

Fresh and Fruity

Strawberry Sensations

Makes: 8 ice pops

Prep: 10 minutes

Freeze: 6–8 hours

Eat: within 3 months of freezing

Kids will go crazy for these wild, colorful, and tasty iced treats – especially if you use fun molds, such as rockets!

* 1¾ cups cranberry juice
* 1 teaspoon finely grated orange rind
* 1 cup sugar syrup (see page 6)
* 6 large strawberries, hulled and cut into thin slices

1. Put the cranberry juice, orange rind, and sugar syrup into a small bowl and stir together well.

2. Pour half of the cranberry mixture into eight ½-cup ice pop molds. (Put the rest of the mixture in the refrigerator, covered.)

3. Drop half of the strawberry slices into the molds, making sure that you have an even number of slices in each one. (Put the rest of the slices in the refrigerator, covered.) Insert the ice pop sticks (see page 8) and freeze for 3–4 hours, or until firm.

4. Pour the remaining cranberry mixture into the molds, then drop in the remaining strawberry slices. Freeze for 3–4 hours, or until firm.

5. To unmold the ice pops, dip the frozen molds into warm water for a few seconds and gently release the pops while holding the sticks.

Blueberry and Pink Lemonade Pops

Makes: 8 ice pops

Prep: 10 minutes

Freeze: 4–5 hours

Eat: within 3 months of freezing

Make these pretty, fruit-filled iced treats for a hot summer's day. Experiment by making them with other berries for more ice pop fun.

* 2 cups pink lemonade, chilled
* juice of ½ lemon
* ½ cup sugar syrup (see page 6)
* 1 cup blueberries

1. Put the pink lemonade, lemon juice, and sugar syrup into a small bowl and stir together well.

2. Drop the blueberries into eight ½-cup ice pop molds, making sure you have an even number of berries in each one.

3. Pour the lemonade mixture over the berries. Insert the ice pop sticks (see page 8) and freeze for 4–5 hours, or until firm.

4. To unmold the ice pops, dip the frozen molds into warm water for a few seconds and gently release the ice pops while holding the sticks.

Summer Melon Medley Pops

Makes: 8 ice pops

Prep: 10 minutes

Freeze: 8 hours

Eat: within 3 months of freezing

Refreshing, cooling, and full of fresh flavors, these melon ice pops will put a smile on anyone's face on a hot summer's day.

* juice and finely grated rind of 1 lime
* ½ cup sugar syrup (see page 6)
* 1 cup seeded and coarsely chopped watermelon flesh
* 1 cup seeded and coarsely chopped cantaloupe melon flesh

1. Put the lime juice, lime rind, and sugar syrup into a small bowl and stir together well.

2. Put the watermelon and half of the lime syrup in a blender and process until smooth. Pour the mixture into eight ½-cup ice pop molds. Freeze for 4 hours, or until firm.

3. When the watermelon mixture is frozen, put the cantaloupe melon and remaining lime syrup in the blender and process until smooth. Pour on top of the frozen watermelon mixture. Insert the ice pop sticks (see page 8) and freeze for 4 hours, or until firm.

4. To unmold the ice pops, dip the frozen molds into warm water for a few seconds and gently release the pops while holding the sticks.

Fruit Cocktail Pops

Makes: 8 ice pops

Prep: 15 minutes

Freeze: 6 hours

Eat: within 3 months of freezing

This is a wonderful way to capture the essence of summer, with the flavors and vibrant colors of ripe, juicy peaches, strawberries, and kiwis.

* 8 ounces strawberries, hulled
* ⅓ cup sugar syrup (see page 6)
* 2 small ripe peaches, peeled, pitted, and coarsely chopped (or 2 cups drained canned peaches)
* 4 large kiwis, peeled and coarsely chopped

1. Put the strawberries in a blender and process until pureed. Stir in 2 tablespoons of the sugar syrup. Pour the mixture into eight ½-cup ice pop molds. Freeze for 2 hours, or until firm.

2. When the strawberry mixture is frozen, put the peaches in the blender and process until pureed. Stir in half of the remaining sugar syrup. Pour over the frozen strawberry mixture. Insert the ice pop sticks (see page 8) and freeze for 2 hours, or until firm.

3. When the peach mixture is frozen, put the kiwis in the blender and process until pureed. Stir in the remaining sugar syrup. Pour over the frozen peach mixture and freeze for 2 hours, or until firm.

4. To unmold the ice pops, dip the frozen molds into warm water for a few seconds and gently release the pops while holding the sticks.

Raspberry and Banana Layer Pops

Makes: 8 ice pops

Prep: 15 minutes

Freeze: 7–8 hours

Eat: within 3 months
of freezing

Creamy vanilla yogurt is pureed with bananas
and honey, then layered with a zingy raspberry
puree, to create a beautiful and delicious ice pop.

* **3 ripe bananas**
* **½ cup vanilla yogurt**
* **½ cup honey**
* **2 cups raspberries**

1. Peel the bananas. Put them in a blender with
the yogurt and half of the honey, then process
until smooth.

2. Pour half of the banana mixture into eight
½-cup ice pop molds. (Put the rest of the mixture
in the refrigerator, covered.) Freeze for 2 hours,
or until firm.

3. When the banana mixture is frozen, put the
raspberries and remaining honey in the blender
and process until pureed. Strain out the seeds using
a fine metal strainer. Pour over the frozen banana
mixture. Insert the ice pop sticks (see page 8) and
freeze for 2 hours, or until firm.

4. Pour the remaining banana mixture over the
frozen raspberry mixture. Freeze for 3–4 hours,
or until firm.

5. To unmold the ice pops, dip the frozen molds into
warm water for a few seconds and gently release
the pops while holding the sticks.

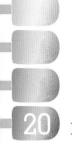

Very Cherry Ripple Pops

Makes: 8 ice pops

Prep: 20 minutes

Cool: 1 hour

Freeze: 4–5 hours

Eat: within 3 months of freezing

Heating the black currants with the sugar and lemon rind intensifies their flavor and works really well with the rich cherry mixture.

* 2 cups black currants or blueberries
* ¼ cup superfine sugar
* finely grated rind of ½ lemon
* ⅓ cup water
* ½ cup cherry preserves
* 1 cup cherry yogurt

1. Put the black currants or blueberries, sugar, lemon rind, and water in a saucepan. Place over medium–low heat, stirring, for 6–8 minutes, or until the sugar has dissolved. Increase the heat to high until the mixture comes to a boil, then reduce the heat to medium and simmer for 5–6 minutes, stirring from time to time. Remove from the heat, cover, and let cool completely; this will take about 1 hour.

2. Process the mixture until smooth using a handheld blender. Transfer to a wide bowl.

3. Put the cherry preserves and yogurt in a separate bowl and, using a metal spoon, beat together until smooth. Gently swirl this mixture into the black currant puree, folding through with a toothpick to create a marbled effect.

4. Spoon the mixture into eight ½-cup ice pop molds. Insert the ice pop sticks (see page 8) and freeze for 4–5 hours, or until firm.

5. To unmold the ice pops, dip the frozen molds into warm water for a few seconds and gently release the pops while holding the sticks.

Pomegranate Power Pops

Makes: 8 ice pops
Prep: 15 minutes
Freeze: 9–10 hours
Eat: within 3 months of freezing

You can buy pomegranate juice for this recipe, but you could also juice fresh pomegranates if you prefer. Simply cut them in half and squeeze the juice through a strainer into a bowl.

* 1 cup pomegranate juice
* 1 cup grapefruit juice
* 1 cup sugar syrup (see page 6)
* ½ cup pomegranate seeds

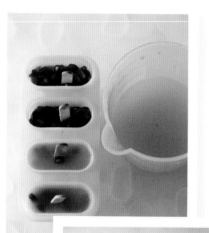

1. Put the pomegranate juice and grapefruit juice into separate small bowls. Pour half of the sugar syrup into each bowl and stir together well.

2. Pour half of the pomegranate mixture into eight ½-cup ice pop molds. (Put the rest of the mixture and the grapefruit mixture in the refrigerator, covered.) Freeze for 2 hours, or until firm.

3. Pour half of the grapefruit mixture over the frozen pomegranate mixture and drop in half of the pomegranate seeds. (Put the rest of the mixture and seeds in the refrigerator, covered.) Insert the ice pop sticks (see page 8) and freeze for 2 hours, or until firm.

4. Pour the remaining pomegranate mixture over the frozen grapefruit mixture and freeze for 2 hours, or until firm.

5. Pour the remaining grapefruit mixture over the frozen pomegranate mixture and drop in the remaining pomegranate seeds. Freeze for 3–4 hours, or until firm.

6. To unmold the ice pops, dip the frozen molds into warm water for a few seconds and gently release the pops while holding the sticks.

Blackberry and Orange Bursts

Makes: 8 ice pops
Prep: 10 minutes
Freeze: 4–5 hours
Eat: within 3 months of freezing

The combination of sweet blackberries, a rich citrus hit, and the deep color of blood orange juice will make these a guaranteed favorite with everyone.

* **2 cups blood orange juice or orange juice**
* **½ cup sugar syrup (see page 6)**
* **2 cups blackberries**

1. Put the blood orange juice and sugar syrup into a small bowl and stir together well.

2. Drop the blackberries into eight ½-cup ice pop molds, making sure you have an even number of berries in each one.

3. Pour the blood orange juice mixture over the berries. Insert the ice pop sticks (see page 8) and freeze for 4–5 hours, or until firm.

4. To unmold the ice pops, dip the frozen molds into warm water for a few seconds and gently release the pops while holding the sticks.

Indulgent

Peaches and Cream Pops

Makes: 8 ice pops
Prep: 15 minutes
Freeze: 6–7 hours
Eat: within 3 months of freezing

Peaches have to be completely ripe and heavy with juice to be enjoyed properly. This is a luxurious iced treat that will delight kids and grown-ups alike.

* ⅓ cup light cream, lightly whipped
* 2 tablespoons confectioners' sugar
* 1 teaspoon vanilla extract
* 4 ripe peaches, peeled, pitted, and coarsely chopped (or 4 cups drained canned peaches)
* ½ cup sugar syrup (see page 6)

1. Put the cream, sugar, and vanilla extract into a small bowl and stir together well.

2. Pour the mixture into eight ½-cup ice pop molds. Freeze for 2 hours, or until firm.

3. When the cream mixture is frozen, put the peaches and sugar syrup in a blender and process until pureed.

4. Pour the peach mixture over the frozen cream mixture. Insert the ice pop sticks (see page 8) and freeze for 4–5 hours, or until firm.

5. To unmold the ice pops, dip the frozen molds into warm water for a few seconds and gently release the pops while holding the sticks.

Choc Berry Rockets

Makes: 8 ice pops

Prep: 25 minutes

Freeze: 4 hours
10 minutes–6 hours
20 minutes

Eat: within 3 months
of freezing

Kids can have fun making these tasty iced treats by dipping them into chocolate and edible sprinkles to create their very own masterpieces.

* 3¼ cups raspberries
* 2 tablespoons lemon juice
* 1 cup sugar syrup (see page 6)
* 8 ounces semisweet dark chocolate, coarsely chopped
* ½ cup sprinkles

1. Put the raspberries, lemon juice, and sugar syrup in a blender and process until pureed. Strain out the seeds using a fine metal strainer. Pour into eight ½-cup ice pop molds. Insert the ice pop sticks (see page 8) and freeze for 3–4 hours, or until firm.

2. When the raspberry mixture is frozen, line a baking sheet with parchment paper. To unmold the ice pops, dip the frozen molds into warm water for a few seconds and gently release the pops while holding the sticks. Place them on the prepared baking sheet and return to the freezer for 1–2 hours.

3. When the ice pops are frozen, put the chocolate in a heatproof bowl, set the bowl over a saucepan of gently simmering water, and heat until melted. Remove from the heat and let cool slightly.

4. Tip the sprinkles onto parchment paper. Dip each ice pop into the melted chocolate so it is covered to about halfway up, then roll it in the sprinkles. Return to the prepared baking sheet and freeze for 10–20 minutes, or until ready to serve.

Mango Fruity Crush Pops

Makes: 8 ice pops
Prep: 20 minutes
Freeze: 6–8 hours
Eat: within 3 months of freezing

These three-layered fruity and creamy treats are packed with color, texture, and flavor. The mango and strawberries work hand-in-hand with the vanilla.

* 1¼ cups mango puree
* ½ cup honey
* 1¼ cups vanilla yogurt
* 2 teaspoons vanilla extract
* 10 ounces strawberries, hulled

1. Put the mango puree and 3 tablespoons of the honey into a small bowl and stir together well.

2. Pour the mixture into eight ½-cup ice pop molds. Freeze for 2 hours, or until firm.

3. When the mango mixture is frozen, put the yogurt, vanilla extract, and another 3 tablespoons of the honey in a bowl and stir together well. Spoon the yogurt mixture over the frozen mango mixture. Insert the ice pop sticks (see page 8) and freeze for 2–3 hours, or until firm.

4. When the vanilla mixture is frozen, put the strawberries and remaining honey in a blender and process until pureed. Strain out the seeds using a fine metal strainer. Pour the puree over the frozen vanilla mixture and freeze for 2–3 hours, or until firm.

5. To unmold the pops, dip the frozen molds into warm water for a few seconds and gently release the pops while holding the sticks.

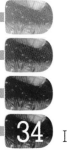

Chocolate Mint Delights

Makes: 8 ice pops
Prep: 25 minutes
Cool: 1 hour
Freeze: 6–8 hours
Eat: within 3 months of freezing

For a kid-friendly version of this chocolate-dipped minty pop, simply omit the crème de menthe and use milk chocolate instead of dark.

* 2 tablespoons crème de menthe
* 1 cup sugar syrup (see page 6)
* 2 cups water
* a small handful of little fresh mint leaves
* 2–3 drops of green food coloring
* 8 ounces semisweet dark chocolate, coarsely chopped

1. Put the crème de menthe, sugar syrup, and water in a saucepan. Place over a medium–high heat until the mixture comes to a boil, stirring. Remove from the heat, cover, and let cool completely; this will take about 1 hour.

2. Stir in the mint leaves and green food coloring and pour into eight ⅓-cup ice pop molds. Insert the ice pop sticks (see page 8) and freeze for 4 hours, or until firm.

3. When the mint mixture is frozen, line a baking sheet with parchment paper. To unmold the ice pops, dip the frozen molds into warm water for a few seconds and gently release the pops while holding the sticks. Place them on the prepared baking sheet and return to the freezer for 1–2 hours.

4. Put the chocolate in a heatproof bowl, set the bowl over a saucepan of gently simmering water, and heat until melted. Remove from the heat and let cool slightly.

5. Dip each ice pop into the melted chocolate so it is covered to one-third of the way up. Return to the prepared baking sheet and freeze for 1–2 hours, or until firm.

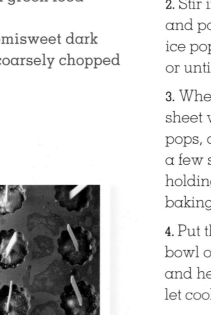

Yogurt Raspberry Ripple Pops

Makes: 8 ice pops

Prep: 15 minutes

Freeze: 4–5 hours

Eat: within 3 months of freezing

The classic combination of raspberries and cream is a guaranteed favorite, and this healthy version, using vanilla yogurt, makes a delicious frozen treat.

* 2 cups raspberries
* ½ cup sugar syrup (see page 6)
* 2 cups vanilla yogurt
* 2 teaspoon vanilla extract

1. Put the raspberries and sugar syrup in a blender and process until smooth. Strain out the seeds using a fine metal strainer. Transfer to a bowl.

2. Put the yogurt and vanilla extract in a bowl and stir together well. Gently swirl this mixture into the raspberry mixture, folding through with a toothpick to create a marbled effect.

3. Spoon the mixture into eight ½-cup ice pop molds. Insert the ice pop sticks (see page 8) and freeze for 4–5 hours, or until firm.

4. To unmold the ice pops, dip the frozen molds into warm water for a few seconds and gently release the pops while holding the sticks.

Triple Chocolate Heaven Pops

Makes: 8 ice pops
Prep: 15 minutes
Cool: 10–12 minutes
Freeze: 3–4 hours
Eat: within 3 months of freezing

For ultimate indulgence, these ice pops will surely hit all the right buttons with their creamy taste and triple chocolate hit.

* 1¼ cups heavy cream
* 4 ounces semisweet dark chocolate, coarsely chopped
* 4 ounces white chocolate, coarsely chopped
* 4 ounces milk chocolate, coarsely chopped

1. Divide the cream equally between three small saucepans. Put the dark chocolate in one pan, the white chocolate in another pan, and the milk chocolate in the final pan.

2. Place each saucepan over a low heat and stir until the chocolate has melted and the mixture is smooth. Remove from the heat and let cool for 10–12 minutes.

3. Pour the dark chocolate mixture into eight ¼-cup ice pop molds. Carefully pour the white chocolate mixture over the dark chocolate, then pour the milk chocolate mixture over the white chocolate. Insert the ice pop sticks (see page 8) and freeze for 3–4 hours, or until firm.

4. To unmold the ice pops, dip the frozen molds into warm water for a few seconds and gently release the pops while holding the sticks.

Banana Split Pops

Makes: 8 ice pops

Prep: 25 minutes

Freeze: 5 hours
10 minutes–6 hours
20 minutes

Eat: within 3 months
of freezing

The delicious chocolate and coconut coating on these ice pops complements the rich, creamy banana mixture that lies within.

* 4 bananas
* ⅓ cup confectioners' sugar
* 2 tablespoons cream of coconut
* ½ cup vanilla yogurt
* 14 ounces semisweet dark chocolate, coarsely chopped
* 1 cup dry sweetened coconut flakes, to decorate

1. Peel the bananas. Put them in a blender with the confectioners' sugar, cream of coconut, and yogurt and process until smooth. Pour the mixture into eight ¼-cup ice pop molds. Insert the ice pop sticks (see page 8) and freeze for 4 hours, or until firm.

2. When the banana mixture is frozen, line a baking sheet with parchment paper. To unmold the ice pops, dip the frozen molds into warm water for a few seconds and gently release the pops while holding the sticks. Place them on the prepared baking sheet and return to the freezer for 1–2 hours.

3. Put the chocolate in a heatproof bowl, set the bowl over a saucepan of gently simmering water, and heat until melted. Remove from the heat and let cool slightly.

4. Dip each ice pop into the melted chocolate, then sprinkle with the dried coconut. Return to the prepared baking sheet and freeze for 10–20 minutes, or until ready to serve.

Dark Chocolate Ripple Pops

Makes: 8 ice pops

Prep: 20 minutes

Freeze: 4–5 hours

Eat: within 3 months of freezing

Chocolate and cream make a classic combination that brings these rippled pops to life, making you want more and more.

* 8 ounces semisweet dark chocolate, coarsely chopped
* 2 cups heavy cream
* ½ cup sugar syrup (see page 6)

1. Put the chocolate and ½ cup of the cream in a small saucepan. Place over a medium–low heat, stirring, until melted and smooth. Remove from the heat and set aside to cool.

2. Meanwhile, pour the remaining cream into a wide bowl and lightly beat with a handheld blender until soft peaks form. Beat in the sugar syrup well.

3. Drizzle the melted chocolate mixture over the cream and fold through using a fork to create a rippled effect.

4. Carefully spoon the mixture into eight ⅓-cup ice pop molds. Insert the ice pop sticks (see page 8) and freeze for 4–5 hours, or until firm.

5. To unmold the ice pops, dip the frozen molds into warm water for a few seconds and gently release the pops while holding the sticks.

New and Zingy

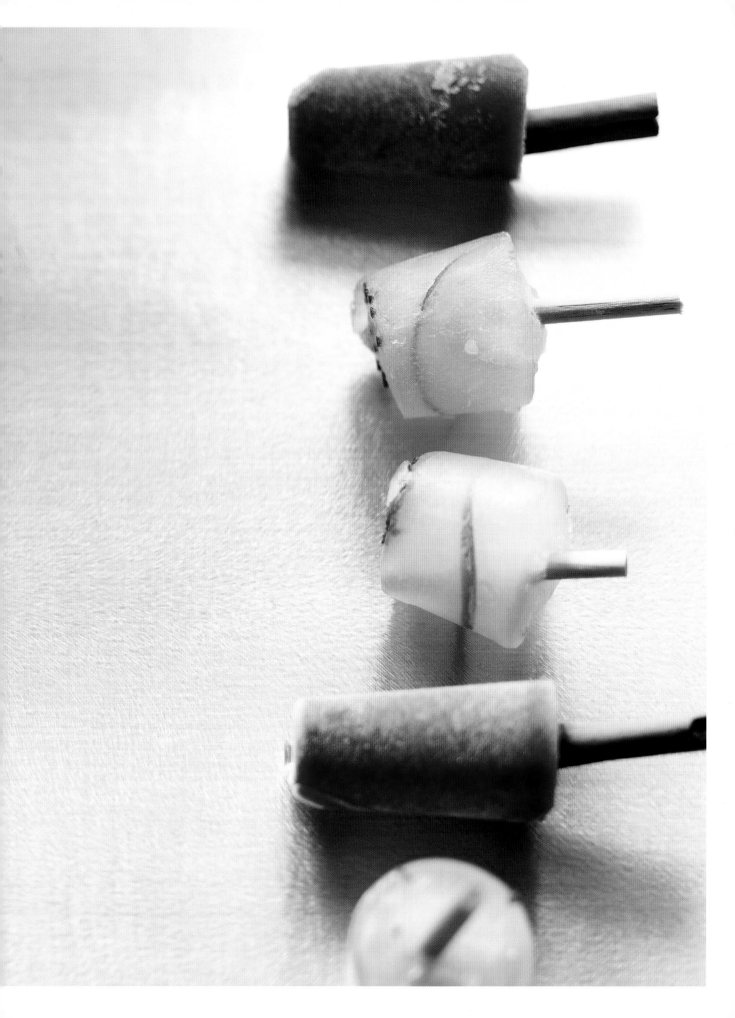

Honeydew Heaven Pops

Makes: 8 ice pops

Prep: 15 minutes

Freeze: 4–5 hours

Eat: within 3 months of freezing

A gorgeously light ice pop; cooling on a hot afternoon and delicious as a dessert after a spicy meal.

* 3½ cups seeded and coarsely chopped honeydew melon flesh
* ½ cup honey
* 1 tablespoon lemongrass paste or finely chopped lemongrass
* ½ cup fresh lemonade
* 8 lemongrass stalks

1. Put the melon, honey, and lemongrass paste in a blender and process until pureed. Add the lemonade and process until smooth.

2. Pour the mixture into eight ½-cup ice pop molds. Insert the lemongrass stalks as sticks (see page 8) and freeze for 4–5 hours, or until firm.

3. To unmold the ice pops, dip the frozen molds into warm water for a few seconds and gently release the pops while holding the lemongrass stalks.

Lime and Chile Sorbet Pops

Makes: 8 ice pops

Prep: 15 minutes

Cool: 1 hour

Freeze: 5–6 hours

Eat: within 3 months of freezing

These pale, chile-speckled sorbet sticks are a twist on the classic lemon sorbet, and have a hidden kick from the chile. For a less spicy version, reduce the amount of chile.

* ½ cup superfine sugar
* 1 red chile, seeded and finely chopped
* 1¾ cups water
* 4 large limes
* 8 thin slices from a small lime

1. Put the sugar, chile, and water in a saucepan. Place over a medium–low heat, stirring, for 6–8 minutes, or until the sugar has dissolved. Increase the heat to medium–high until the mixture comes to a boil, then remove from the heat.

2. Finely grate the rind of 2 of the limes into the mixture and stir. Cover and let cool completely; this will take about 1 hour.

3. Squeeze the juice from the 4 limes and stir it into the mixture.

4. Pour the mixture into eight ¼-cup ice pop molds and place a lime slice into each mold. Insert the ice pop sticks (see page 8) and freeze for 5–6 hours, or until firm.

5. To unmold the ice pops, dip the frozen molds into warm water for a few seconds and gently release the pops while holding the sticks.

Watermelon Chill-Out Pops

Makes: 8 ice pops

Prep: 10 minutes

Freeze: 6 hours

Eat: within 3 months of freezing

Basil and watermelon are a wonderful combination when brought together in this colorful iced treat.

* 3½ cups seeded and coarsely chopped watermelon flesh
* ½ cup sugar syrup (see page 6)
* 1 tablespoon finely chopped fresh basil leaves
* finely grated rind of 1 lime
* 16 small–medium fresh basil leaves

1. Put the watermelon, sugar syrup, chopped basil, and lime rind in a blender and process until pureed and flecked.

2. Put 2 basil leaves into each of eight ⅓-cup ice pop molds. Pour the watermelon mixture into the molds. Insert the ice pop sticks (see page 8) and freeze for 6 hours, or until firm.

3. To unmold the ice pops, dip the frozen molds into warm water for a few seconds and gently release the pops while holding the sticks.

Spiced Plum Pops

Makes: 8 ice pops

Prep: 15 minutes

Cool: 1 hour

Freeze: 5 hours

Eat: within 3 months of freezing

This plum-and-spice mixture is bursting with late summer flavors, but with warming spice in the background.

* 6 ripe plums, peeled, halved, pitted, and sliced
* 1 teaspoon ground cinnamon
* a pinch of ground cloves
* a pinch of ground star anise
* ⅓ cup superfine sugar
* ½ cup water
* juice of 1 orange
* 8 cinnamon sticks

1. Put the plums, cinnamon, cloves, star anise, sugar, and water in a saucepan. Place over a medium heat, stirring, for 6–8 minutes, or until the sugar has dissolved. Increase the heat to high until the mixture comes to a boil, then reduce the heat to medium and simmer for 4–5 minutes, stirring from time to time.

2. Transfer the mixture to a blender, add the orange juice, then process until pureed. Let cool completely; this will take about 1 hour.

3. Pour the mixture into eight ¼-cup ice pop molds. Insert the cinnamon sticks (see page 8) and freeze for 5 hours, or until firm.

4. To unmold the ice pops, dip the frozen molds into warm water for a few seconds and gently release the pops while holding the cinnamon sticks.

Coconut Passion Pops

Makes: 8 ice pops

Prep: 15 minutes

Cool: 1 hour

Freeze: 5–7 hours

Eat: within 3 months
of freezing

The tropical flavors of pineapple, passion fruit, and coconut make them natural partners in these refreshing and creamy ice pops.

* juice and pulp of 5 large passion fruit (about ⅔ cup)
* 1 cup sugar syrup (see page 6)
* ⅔ cup chopped pineapple flesh
* ¾ cup half-and-half
* ⅔ cup heavy cream
* ¼ teaspoon coconut extract

1. Put the passion fruit juice and pulp in a small saucepan with half of the sugar syrup. Place over a medium–high heat, stirring, until the mixture comes to a boil. Remove from the heat, cover, and let cool completely; this will take about 1 hour.

2. Pour the mixture into eight ½-cup ice pop molds and freeze for 2–3 hours, or until firm.

3. When the passion fruit mixture is frozen, put the pineapple, half-and-half, heavy cream, coconut extract, and remaining sugar syrup in a blender and process until fairly smooth. Pour the pineapple mixture over the frozen passion fruit mixture. Insert the ice pop sticks (see page 8) and freeze for 3–4 hours, or until firm.

4. To unmold the ice pops, dip the frozen molds into warm water for a few seconds and gently release the pops while holding the sticks.

Milky Chai Pops

Makes: 8 ice pops

Prep: 15 minutes

Steep and cool:
2½ hours

Freeze: 5–6 hours

Eat: within 3 months
of freezing

Full of spicy, Eastern flavors, this popular drink makes a great iced dessert and is sure to quickly become a household favorite.

* 1 cup milk
* 1 star anise
* 10 cloves
* 3 cinnamon sticks
* 10 white peppercorns
* 6 cardamom pods, lightly crushed
* 1¼ cups water
* 2 tablespoons black tea leaves (Ceylon or English breakfast)
* ½ cup sweetened condensed milk

1. Put the milk, star anise, cloves, cinnamon, white peppercorns, cardamom pods, and water in a saucepan. Place over a medium–high heat and bring to a boil, stirring. Remove from the heat and let steep for 40–50 minutes to infuse the flavors of the spices.

2. Return the pan to the heat and bring to a boil, stirring. Add the tea leaves, remove from the heat, stir well, and let steep for 10–15 minutes.

3. Pour through a fine metal strainer into a bowl and discard the tea and spices. Stir in the condensed milk and let cool completely.

4. Pour the mixture into eight ½-cup ice pop molds. Insert the ice pop sticks (see page 8) and freeze for 5–6 hours, or until firm.

5. To unmold the ice pops, dip the frozen molds into warm water for a few seconds and gently release the pops while holding the sticks.

Cappuccino Pops

Makes: 8 ice pops

Prep: 15 minutes

Cool: 30 minutes

Freeze: 6–7 hours

Eat: within 3 months of freezing

Coffee made from freshly ground beans is a superb flavoring for any iced dessert. Instant coffee works, too, but the flavor will be less intense.

* ⅔ cup sweetened condensed milk
* ½ cup heavy cream
* 2½ cups brewed espresso coffee, at room temperature
* 1 tablespoon unsweetened cocoa powder

1. Put ¼ cup of the condensed milk into a small bowl with the heavy cream and lightly beat until well combined and slightly thickened.

2. Pour the mixture into eight ½-cup ice pop molds and freeze for 2 hours, or until firm.

3. Meanwhile, beat the remaining condensed milk with the coffee and cocoa powder in a bowl until well blended. Let cool completely.

4. Pour the coffee mixture over the frozen cream mixture. Insert the ice pop sticks (see page 8) and freeze for 4–5 hours, or until firm.

5. To unmold the ice pops, dip the frozen molds into warm water for a few seconds and gently release the pops while holding the sticks.

Pops with a Kick

OVER 21 ONLY

Strawberry Margarita Pops

Makes: 8 ice pops

Prep: 10 minutes

Freeze: 6–8 hours

Eat: within 3 months
of freezing

Seriously fruity, but with a light boozy kick, these pops add a Mexican flamboyance to any party.

* 3 cups hulled and chopped strawberries
* ½ cup sugar syrup (see page 6)
* juice and finely grated rind of 1 lime
* 2 tablespoons tequila
* 1 tablespoon Cointreau
* a pinch of salt
* ⅔ cup water
* 2 tablespoons superfine sugar, to serve

1. Put all the ingredients except the superfine sugar into a blender and process until smooth.

2. Pour the mixture into eight ⅓-cup ice pop molds. Insert the ice pop sticks (see page 8) and freeze for 6–8 hours, or until firm.

3. To unmold the ice pops, dip the frozen molds into warm water for a few seconds and gently release the pops while holding the sticks.

4. To serve the ice pops, place the superfine sugar on a plate and dip the ice pops in the sugar.

Peach Bellini Pops

Makes: 8 ice pops

Prep: 15 minutes

Freeze: 8–10 hours

Eat: within 3 months of freezing

The ultimate Italian summer flavor experience, these heady iced treats will have your guests coming back for more.

* 2 ripe peaches, peeled, pitted, and cut into small dice
* 2 tablespoons peach liqueur
* 1¼ cups prosecco
* 1 cup sugar syrup (see page 6)

1. Divide the peaches between eight ¼-cup ice pop molds or plastic Champagne glasses.

2. Put the peach liqueur, prosecco, and sugar syrup into a small bowl and stir together well.

3. Pour the mixture into the molds or plastic glasses. Insert the ice pop sticks (see page 8) and freeze for 8–10 hours, or until firm.

4. To unmold the ice pops, wrap the frozen molds or plastic glasses in a hot water-soaked dish towel for a few seconds and gently release the pops while holding the sticks.

Apple Martini Pops

Makes: 8 ice pops

Prep: 10 minutes

Freeze: 8–10 hours

Eat: within 3 months
of freezing

These "cocktails on a stick" are a great summer treat!
Apple and lemon rind give a twist to the classic Martini.

* 1¾ cups apple juice
* ½ cup sugar syrup (see page 6)
* finely grated rind of 1 lemon
* 3 tablespoons gin
* 1 tablespoon dry vermouth
* 8 thin, small apple slices

1. Put all the ingredients except the apple slices into a small bowl and stir together well.

2. Pour the mixture into eight ⅓-cup ice pop molds or plastic Martini glasses. Drop an apple slice into each mold or plastic glass. Insert the ice pop sticks or plastic cocktail sticks (see page 8) and freeze for 8–10 hours, or until firm.

3. To unmold the ice pops, wrap the frozen molds or plastic glasses in a hot water-soaked dish towel for a few seconds and gently release the pops while holding the sticks.

Mojito Pops

Makes: 8 ice pops

Prep: 15 minutes

Freeze: 10–12 hours

Eat: within 3 months
of freezing

Get your mojito fix in an ice pop. Now you can cool down with one of your favorite drinks and never worry about getting your glass mixed up with someone else's! For a child-friendly version, simply leave out the rum.

* juice of 6 limes
* 2½ cups chilled club soda
* leaves from 1 bunch of fresh mint
* 3 limes, cut into wedges
* ½ cup superfine sugar
* 2 tablespoons white rum

1. Put the lime juice and club soda into a small bowl and stir together well.

2. Stir in the mint leaves, lime wedges, sugar, and rum. Using a "muddler," thick wooden spoon, or mallet, mash together all the ingredients until well blended.

3. Pour the mixture into eight ½-cup ice pop molds. Divide the lime wedges and mint leaves evenly among them. Insert the ice pop sticks (see page 8) and freeze for 10–12 hours, or until firm.

4. To unmold the ice pops, dip the frozen molds into warm water for a few seconds and gently release the pops while holding the sticks.

Pina Colada Pops

Makes: 8 ice pops

Prep: 15 minutes

Freeze: 6–8 hours

Eat: within 3 months
of freezing

The cool and refreshing combination of pineapple, coconut, and rum will delight grown-up ice pop lovers. A perfect way to beat the summer heat, these are elegant enough to impress and much too delicious to resist.

* 3½ cups finely diced pineapple flesh
* 1 cup coconut milk
* ⅓ cup superfine sugar
* 2 tablespoons Malibu

1. Drop a tablespoon of the diced pineapple flesh into each of eight ½-cup ice pop molds.

2. Put the remaining pineapple flesh in a blender with the coconut milk, sugar, and Malibu and process until smooth.

3. Strain using a fine metal strainer, pressing down to extract all the juice. Discard the solids. Pour the mixture into the ice pop molds. Insert the ice pop sticks (see page 8) and freeze for 6–8 hours, or until firm.

4. To unmold the ice pops, dip the frozen molds into warm water for a few seconds and gently release the pops while holding the sticks.

Gin and Tonic Pops

Makes: 8 ice pops

Prep: 10 minutes

Freeze: 6–8 hours

Eat: within 3 months of freezing

A naughty yet refreshing grown-up ice pop for a hot summer's day – ideal for sharing in the early evening, as the sun goes down.

* 1 cup sugar syrup (see page 6)
* 2 tablespoons gin
* 1¾ cups tonic water
* juice of 1 lime
* 16 thin, small cucumber slices

1. Put the sugar syrup, gin, tonic water, and lime juice into a small bowl and stir together well.

2. Pour the mixture into eight ⅓-cup ice pop molds. Drop 2 slices of cucumber into each mold. Insert the ice pop sticks (see page 8) and freeze for 6–8 hours, or until firm.

3. To unmold the ice pops, dip the frozen molds into warm water for a few seconds and gently release the pops while holding the sticks.

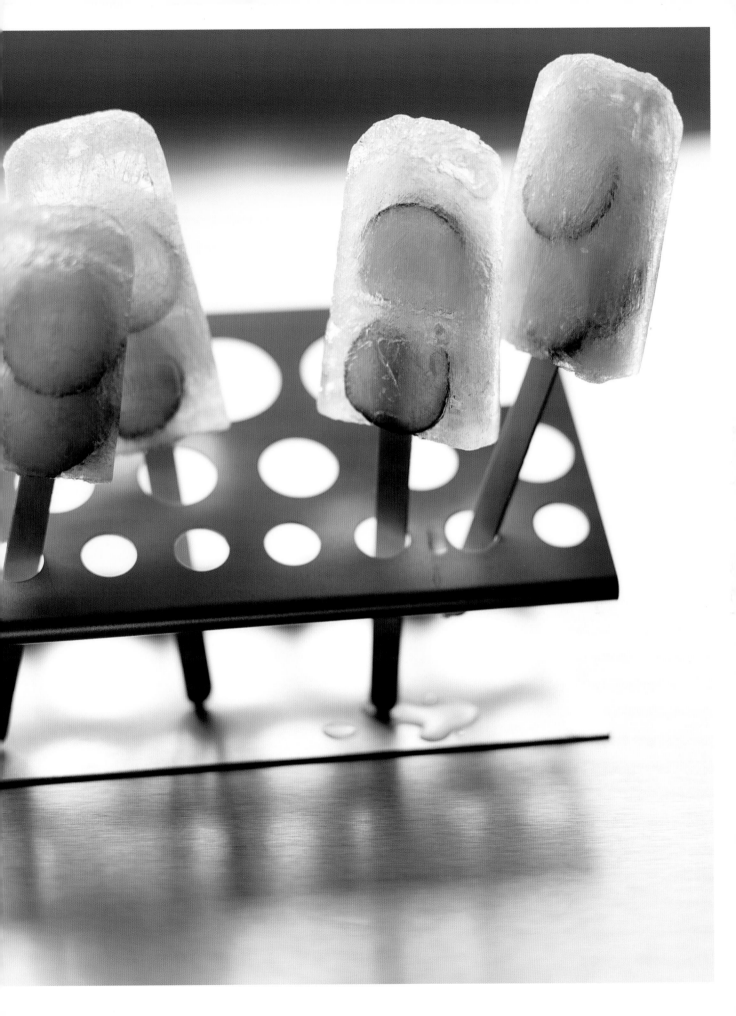

Cosmopolitan Pops

Makes: 8 ice pops

Prep: 10 minutes

Freeze: 8–10 hours

Eat: within 3 months
of freezing

Make these colorful and lightly alcoholic pops to serve
at the end of a long summer lunch. Keep in the freezer
until the last minute, and for impressive entertaining,
serve them on a tray filled with ice cubes or crushed ice.

* 1 cup sugar syrup (see page 6)
* 2 cups cranberry juice
* 2 tablespoons vodka
* 1 tablespoon Cointreau
* juice of 1 lime
* finely grated rind
  of 1 clementine

1. Put all the ingredients into a small bowl
and stir well.

2. Pour the mixture into eight ½-cup ice pop molds.
Insert the ice pop sticks (see page 8) and freeze for
8–10 hours, or until firm.

3. To unmold the ice pops, dip the frozen molds into
warm water for a few seconds and gently release
the pops while holding the sticks.

Black Russian Pops

Dark and decadent, these smooth ice pops make a great after-dinner treat on a hot summer's night.

* 1 tablespoon Kahlua or Tia Maria
* 2 cups cola
* 2 tablespoons vodka

1. Put all the ingredients into a small bowl and stir together well.

2. Pour the mixture into eight ¼-cup ice pop molds or thick shot glasses. Insert the ice pop sticks (see page 8) and freeze for 8–10 hours, or until firm.

3. To unmold the ice pops, wrap the frozen molds or glasses in a hot water-soaked dish towel for a few seconds and gently release the pops while holding the sticks.

Index